LOL

JOHNNY B. LAUGHING

Johnny B. Laughing, The Joke King

Copyright © 2017. All rights reserved.

This book is a work of fiction. No part of this book or this book as a whole may be used, reproduced, or transmitted in any form or means without written permission from the publisher.

Published by Hey Sup Bye Publishing.

Created in the U.S.A.

ISBN: 9781973333197

DEDICATION

THIS BOOK IS DEDICATED TO YOU,
THE READER. IT'S A REAL PLEASURE
CREATING THESE SILLY JOKE BOOKS
FOR YOU TO ENJOY. SHARE THE
GIFT OF LAUGHTER WITH A FRIEND!

TABLE OF CONTENTS

FUNNY JOKES

Q: WHAT DO YOU CALL A BORING DOG?

A: A DULL-MATION!

Q: WHAT DO YOU CALL A CAT THAT CAN HOP OVER A WALL?

A: A GOOD JUMPURR!

Q: WHY DO COWS LIKE JOKES?

A: BECAUSE THEY LIKE BEING AMOOOOOSED!

Q: WHAT'S A SEA SERPENT'S FAVORITE MEAL?

A: FISH AND SHIPS!

Q: WHAT DID THE MONKEY LEARN IN SCHOOL?

A: THE APEY-CEES!

Q: WHAT DO YOU CALL A PIG THAT STEALS?

A: PIG POCKET!

Q: WHY ARE FROGS SO HAPPY?

A: THEY EAT WHATEVER BUGS THEM!

Q: HOW DO YOU MAKE AN APPLE TURNOVER?

A: PUSH IT DOWNHILL!

Q: WHY DO ELEPHANTS EAT RAW FOOD?

A: BECAUSE THEY DON'T KNOW HOW TO COOK!

Q: WHAT DO YOU GET WHEN YOU CROSS A BOMB AND A DINOSAUR?

A: DINO-MITE!

LOL

Q: WHAT DO YOU SAY TO A TOAD?

A: WARTS NEW?

Q: WHAT DO YOU GET IF YOU CROSS A DUCK WITH A FIREWORK?

A: A FIREQUACKER!

Q: WHAT DID THE CAT SAY TO THE FISH?

A: I'VE GOT A BONE TO PICK WITH YOU!

Q: WHAT FISH MAKE THE BEST SANDWICHES?

A: A PEANUT BUTTER AND JELLYFISH!

Q: WHY DID THE GORILLA FAIL ENGLISH?

A: HE HAD LITTLE APE-TITUDE!

Q: WHY WOULDN'T ANYONE PLAY WITH THE LITTLE LONGHORN?

A: HE WAS TOO MUCH OF A BULLY!

Q: WHAT IS A GHOST'S FAVORITE FRUIT?

A: BOONANA!

Q: WHAT'S A DOG'S FAVORITE HOBBY?

A: COLLECTING FLEAS!

Q: WHY DID THE TURKEY CROSS THE ROAD?

A: TO PROVE HE WASN'T CHICKEN!

Q: WHY DID THE PIG MAKE BAD GRADES?

A: HE WAS A SLOW LOINER!

Q: WHAT DINOSAUR CAN'T STAY OUT IN THE RAIN?

A: STEGOSAUR-RUST!

Q: WHAT DO YOU GET IF CROSS A FROG WITH SOME MIST?

A: KERMIT THE FOG!

Q: HOW DOES AN ELEPHANT GET OUT OF A SMALL CAR?

A: THE SAME WAY THAT HE GOT IN!

Q: WHERE DO FISH SLEEP?

A: IN A RIVERBED!

Q: WHY DID THE CHICKEN CROSS THE BASKETBALL COURT?

A: HE HEARD THE REFEREE CALLING FOWLS!

Q: WHEN IS IT UNLUCKY TO SEE A BLACK CAT?

A: WHEN YOU'RE A MOUSE!

Q: WHY DID THE BANANA GO OUT WITH THE PRUNE?

A: BECAUSE HE COULDN'T FIND A DATE!

Q: WHY ARE GORILLAS UNDERPAID?

A: THEY'RE WILLING TO WORK FOR PEANUTS!

Q: WHAT DO YOU CALL A LITTER OF YOUNG DOGS IN THE SNOW?

A: SLUSH PUPPIES!

Q: WHY DID THE PIG GO TO THE CASINO?

A: TO PLAY THE SLOP MACHINE!

Q: WHY ARE FISH SO BAD AT TENNIS?

A: THEY DON'T LIKE TO GET TOO CLOSE TO THE NET!

Q: WHAT DO FROGS DRINK?

A: HOT CROAKO!

Q: WHY DON'T COWS EVER HAVE ANY MONEY?

A: BECAUSE THE FARMERS MILK THEM DRY!

Q: WHAT KIND OF ELEPHANT LIVES IN ANTARCTICA?

A: COLD ONES!

Q: WHAT WOULD YOU GET IF YOU CROSSED A DINOSAUR AND A PIG?

A: JURASSIC PORK!

Q: WHAT DO YOU GIVE A SICK BIRD?

A: TWEETMENT!

Q: WHY DID THE ROOSTER RUN AWAY?

A: HE WAS A CHICKEN!

Q: HOW DO YOU TUNE A FISH?

A: WITH ITS SCALES!

Q: WHAT KIND OF SHOES DO FROGS WEAR?

A: OPEN TOAD SANDALS!

Q: WHY DO DOGS RUN IN CIRCLES?

A: BECAUSE IT'S HARD TO RUN IN SQUARES!

Q: WHY AREN'T BURGERS ANY GOOD AT BASKETBALL?

A: TOO MANY TURNOVERS!

Q: WHAT DOES A CAT CALL A BOWL OF MICE?

A: THE PURRFECT MEAL!

Q: WHERE DO PIGS GO TO PLAY IN NEW YORK CITY?

A: CENTRAL PORK!

Q: WHY DID THE DOG JUMP INTO THE POND?

A: HE WANTED TO CHASE THE CATFISH!

Q: WHY DID THE FARMER FEED MONEY TO HIS COWS?

A: HE WANTED RICH MILK!

Q: WHAT TYPE OF TOOL DID THE CAVE MEN USE?

A: A DINO-SAW!

Q: HOW DO YOU COMMUNICATE WITH A FISH?

A: YOU DROP IT A LINE!

Q: WHAT KIND OF BUSINESS IS KING KONG IN?

A: MONKEY BUSINESS!

Q: WHERE DO BIRDS INVEST THEIR MONEY?

A: IN THE STORK MARKET!

Q: WHAT IS WORSE THAN A DOG HOWLING AT THE MOON?

A: TWO DOGS HOWLING AT THE MOON!

Q: WHY DID THE CAT PUT THE LETTER M INTO THE FREEZER?

A: BECAUSE IT TURNS ICE INTO MICE!

Q: WHY DID THE COW JUMP OVER THE MOON?

A: TO GET TO THE MILKY WAY!

Q: WHY ARE FISH SO GULLIBLE?

A: THEY ALWAYS FALL FOR HOOK, LINE, AND SINKER!

Q: WHAT DO YOU CALL A DINOSAUR WITH A LARGE VOCABULARY?

A: A THESAURUS!

Q: WHERE DO NAUGHTY PIGS GO?

A: THEY GET SENT TO THE PEN!

Q: WHAT KIND OF HORSE CAN SWIM UNDERWATER WITHOUT COMING UP FOR AIR?

A: A SEAHORSE!

Q: WHAT KIND OF BIRDS DO YOU USUALLY FIND LOCKED UP?

A: JAIL BIRDS!

Q: WHAT DO YOU CALL A DOG IN THE MIDDLE OF A MUDDY ROAD?

A: A MUTT IN A RUT!

Q: WHAT KIND OF MOVIE DOES A RABBIT LIKE BEST?

A: ONE WITH A HOPPY ENDING!

Q: WHICH FISH DRESSES THE BEST?

A: A SWORDFISH BECAUSE IT ALWAYS LOOKS SHARP!

Q: WHAT HAPPENED WHEN THE OWL LOST HIS VOICE?

A: HE DIDN'T GIVE A HOOT!

Q: WHAT DINOSAUR WOULD YOU FIND IN A RODEO?

A: BRONCO-SAURUS!

Q: WHAT DO YOU SAY TO A HITCHHIKING FROG?

A: HOP IN!

Q: HOW IS CAT FOOD SOLD?

A: PURR CAN!

Q: WHY DO HAMBURGERS MAKE GOOD BASEBALL PLAYERS?

A: THEY'RE GREAT AT THE PLATE!

Q: WHAT IS SMARTER THAN A TALKING CAT?

A: A SPELLING BEE!

Q: WHAT HAPPENED WHEN THE DOG WENT TO THE FLEA CIRCUS?

A: IT STOLE THE SHOW!

Q: WHAT'S THE HARDEST THING ABOUT LEARNING TO RIDE A HORSE?

A: THE GROUND!

Q: WHERE DO THE MOST ATHLETIC PIGS COMPETE EVERY FOUR YEARS?

A: THE OLYMPIGS!

Q: DID YOU HEAR ABOUT THE FORGETFUL SNAKE?

A: HE LOST HIS SKIN!

Q: WHAT DO YOU CALL A RABBIT
WHO TELLS JOKES?

A: A FUNNY BUNNY!

Q: WHERE DO COWS GO TO DANCE?

A: TO THE MEAT BALL!

Q: WHERE DO FISH COME FROM?

A: FINLAND!

Q: WHAT HAPPENS WHEN DUCKS FLY UPSIDE DOWN?

A: THEY QUACK UP!

Q: WHERE DO MILK SHAKES COME FROM?

A: NERVOUS COWS!

Q: WHERE DO YOU TAKE A SICK HORSE?

A: TO THE HORSPITAL!

Q: HOW DOES A BURGER ACQUIRE GOOD TASTE?

A: WITH A LITTLE SEASONING!

Q: WHAT DO YOU CALL A DINOSAUR WEARING TIGHT SHOES?

A: MY-FEET-ARE-SORE-US!

Q: WHAT KIND OF DOG DOES DRACULA LIKE?

A: A BLOODHOUND!

Q: WHAT KIND OF MONEY DO FISHERMEN MAKE?

A: NET PROFITS!

Q: WHAT'S LONG, GREEN, AND GOES HITH?

A: A SNAKE WITH A LISP!

Q: WHAT DO YOU CALL AN EASY-GOING RABBIT?

A: HOPPY-GO-LUCKY!

Q: WHAT DO YOU GET IF YOU CROSS A CAT WITH SANTA?

A: SANTA CLAWS!

Q: WHAT IS A PIG'S BEST KARATE MOVE?

A: PORK CHOP!

Q: WHAT DID THE HAMBURGER SAY WHEN IT PLEADED NOT GUILTY?

A: I'VE BEEN FLAMED!

Q: WHAT DO YOU GET WHEN A CHICKEN LAYS AN EGG ON TOP OF A BARN?

A: AN EGGROLL!

Q: WHAT IS THE STRONGEST BIRD?

A: A CRANE!

Q: WHY DID THE MOTHER CAT PUT STAMPS ON HER KITTENS?

A: BECAUSE SHE WANTED TO MAIL A LITTER!

Q: WHAT KIND OF DOG IS A PERSON'S BEST FRIEND?

A: A PALMATIAN!

Q: WHY DID THE HORSE MISS THE JOUST?

A: HE HAD THE KNIGHT OFF!

Q: WHAT DO YOU GIVE A SICK PIG?

A: OINKMENT!

Q: WHY ARE FISH SO SMART?

A: THEY ARE ALWAYS IN SCHOOLS!

Q: WHAT DO YOU CALL A PREHISTORIC MONSTER WHEN IT SLEEPS?

A: A DINO-SNORE!

Q: WHERE CAN A BURGER GET GOOD NIGHT'S SLEEP?

A: ON A BED OF LETTUCE!

Q: WHERE DO RUSSIAN BULLS COME FROM?

A: MOSCOW!

Q: WHAT DO YOU CALL IT WHEN A CAT STOPS?

A: A PAWS!

Q: WHAT DO YOU CALL AN UNIQUE RABBIT?

A: A RARE HARE!

Q: WHAT'S THE BEST THING ABOUT DEADLY SNAKES?

A: THEY'VE GOT POISONALITY!

Q: WHAT DO CHICKENS SERVE AT BIRTHDAY PARTIES?

A: COOP CAKES!

Q: WHAT KIND OF DOG CHASES ANYTHING RED?

A: A BULL DOG!

Q: WHAT FISH ONLY SWIMS AT NIGHT?

A: A STARFISH!

Q: HOW MUCH MONEY DID THE HORSE HAVE?

A: ONLY A BUCK!

Q: WHAT DO YOU CALL A FAKE NOODLE?

A: AN IMPASTA!

Q: WHY WAS THE MOTHER FLEA SO UNHAPPY?

A: ALL HER CHILDREN HAVE GONE TO THE DOGS!

Q: WHERE DO BABY COWS EAT?

A: AT THE CALF-ATERIA!

Q: WHY DID THE DINOSAUR CROSS THE ROAD?

A: BECAUSE THE CHICKEN WASN'T INVENTED YET!

Q: WHAT DO YOU CALL THE EVERYDAY ROUTINES OF A RABBIT?

A: RABBIT HABITS!

Q: WHAT SUBJECT ARE SNAKES GOOD AT IN SCHOOL?

A: HISS-TORY!

Q: WHAT DO YOU CALL AN EGG FROM OUTER SPACE?

A: AN UNIDENTIFIED FLYING OMELET!

Q: WHAT DO YOU CALL A PONY WITH A SORE THROAT?

A: A LITTLE HOARSE!

Q: WHAT HAPPENED TO THE DOG THAT ATE NOTHING BUT GARLIC?

A: HIS BARK WAS MUCH WORSE THAN HIS BITE!

Q: IS CHICKEN SOUP GOOD FOR YOUR HEALTH?

A: NOT IF YOU'RE THE CHICKEN!

Q: WHAT WOULD YOU HEAR AT A COW CONCERT?

A: MOO-SIC!

Q: WHAT DO YOU CALL A PIG WITH NO LEGS?

A: A GROUNDHOG!

Q: WHAT DOES A RABBIT USE TO KEEP HIS FUR NEAT?

A: A HAREBRUSH!

Q: WHY DON'T CHICKENS LIKE PEOPLE?

A: THEY BEAT EGGS!

Q: HOW LONG DO CHICKENS WORK?

A: AROUND THE CLUCK!

Q: WHAT DID THE DOG SAY WHEN HE SAT ON SANDPAPER?

A: RUFF!

Q: WHAT'S A SNAKE'S FAVORITE DANCE?

A: SNAKE, RATTLE, AND ROLL!

Q: WHAT DO YOU GIVE A SICK HORSE?

A: COUGH STIRRUP!

Q: WHY DID THE COOKIE GO TO THE DOCTOR?

A: HE WAS FEELING CRUMMY!

Q: WHAT DO YOU CALL IT WHEN TWO DINOSAURS GET IN A CAR ACCIDENT?

A: TYRANNOSAURUS WRECKS!

Q: WHAT'S A RABBIT'S FAVORITE SONG?

A: HOPPY BIRTHDAY TO YOU!

Q: WHAT FOOD IS GOOD FOR THE BRAIN?

A: NOODLE SOUP!

Q: WHAT KIND OF COWS DO YOU FIND IN ALASKA?

A: ESKI-MOOS!

Q: WHERE DOES A FISH GO TO BORROW MONEY?

A: THE LOAN SHARK!

Q: WHAT DO PIGS DRIVE?

A: PIG-UP TRUCKS!

Q: HOW DO YOU GET A DOG TO STOP BARKING IN THE BACK SEAT OF A CAR?

A: PUT HIM IN THE FRONT SEAT!

Q: WHAT IS EVERY CAT'S FAVORITE SONG?

A: THREE BLIND MICE!

Q: WHAT HAPPENED TO THE HORSE THAT SWALLOWED A DOLLAR BILL?

A: IT BUCKED!

Q: WHAT U.S. STATE HAS THE MOST COWS?

A: MOOSOURI!

Q: WHY DID THE CHICKEN CROSS THE PLAYGROUND?

A: TO GET TO THE OTHER SLIDE!

Q: WHICH GAME DID THE CAT WANT TO PLAY WITH THE MOUSE?

A: CATCH!

Q: WHERE DO RABBITS GO AFTER THEY GET MARRIED?

A: ON THEIR BUNNYMOON!

Q: WHAT IS BLACK AND WHITE AND RED ALL OVER?

A: A DALMATIAN WITH A SUNBURN!

Q: WHAT DO YOU GET IF YOU CROSS AN ALIEN AND A HOT DRINK?

A: GRAVI-TEA!

Q: WHAT HAPPENS WHEN A COW STOPS SHAVING?

A: IT GROWS A MOOSTACHE!

Q: WHAT DID ONE PLATE SAY TO THE OTHER PLATE?

A: LUNCH IS ON ME!

Q: HOW DO YOU TAKE A PIG TO THE HOSPITAL?

A: IN A HAMBULANCE!

Q: WHICH BIG CAT SHOULD YOU NEVER PLAY CARDS WITH?

A: A CHEETAH!

Q: WHERE DID THE DUCK GO WHEN HE GOT SICK?

A: THE DUCKTOR!

Q: WHAT DO YOU GET IF YOU CROSS A STEER AND A CHICKEN?

A: ROOST BEEF!

Q: DID YOU HEAR ABOUT THE HORSE WITH A NEGATIVE ALTITUDE?

A: HE ALWAYS SAID NAY!

Q: WHAT DO YOU CALL A COW LYING IN THE GRASS?

A: GROUND BEEF!

Q: WHAT FISH IS BEST TO HAVE IN A BOAT?

A: A SAILFISH!

Q: WHICH DOG CAN TELL TIME?

A: A WATCHDOG!

Q: WHY IS A BUNNY THE LUCKIEST ANIMAL IN THE WORLD?

A: BECAUSE IT HAS FOUR RABBIT'S FEET!

Q: WHAT'S RED AND GREEN AND WEARS BOXING GLOVES?

A: FRUIT PUNCH!

Q: WHAT DO COWS GET WHEN THEY ARE SICK?

A: HAY FEVER!

Q: WHAT WAS THE MOST FLEXIBLE DINOSAUR?

A: TYRANNOSAURUS FLEX!

Q: HOW DOES A COW DO MATH?

A: WITH A COWCULATOR!

ABOUT THE AUTHOR

The Joke King, Johnny B. Laughing is a best-selling joke book author. He is a jokester at heart and enjoys a good laugh, pulling pranks on his friends, and telling funny and hilarious jokes!

FOR MORE FUNNY JOKE BOOKS JUST SEARCH FOR "JOHNNY B. LAUGHING" ON AMAZON

-OR-

VISIT THE WEBSITE: WWW.FUNNY-JOKES-ONLINE.WEEBLY.COM

JOHNNY B. LAUGHING

Printed in Poland
by Amazon Fulfillment
Poland Sp. z o.o., Wrocław